Exercising Influence Workbook:

A Self-Study Guide

B. Kim Barnes

Pfeiffer
A Wiley Imprint
www.pfeiffer.com

Published by Pfeiffer
An Imprint of Wiley
989 Market Street, San Francisco, CA 94103-1741

www.pfeiffer.com

For additional copies/bulk purchases of this book in the U.S. please contact 800-274-4434.

Pfeiffer books and products are available through most bookstores. To contact Pfeiffer directly call our Customer Care Department within the U.S. at 800-274-4434, outside the U.S. at 317-572-3985, fax 317-572-4002, or visit www.pfeiffer.com.

Pfeiffer also publishes its books in a variety of electronic formats. Some content that appears in print may not be available in electronic books.

ISBN-10: 0-7879-8465-5

ISBN-13: 978-0-7879-8465-6

Acquiring Editor: Lisa Shannon
Director of Development: Kathleen Dolan Davies
Production Editor: Dawn Kilgore
Editor: Rebecca Taff
Manufacturing Supervisor: Becky Carreño

Printed in the United States of America

Printing   10   9   8   7   6   5   4   3   2   1

Contents

Introduction

THIS WORKBOOK is intended to accompany the book, *Exercising Influence.* You can use it in several ways:

- After reading the book, to apply the concepts and tools to an upcoming influence opportunity

- As you are reading the book, to clarify the concepts and tools by applying each chapter's ideas to a real situation

- Several weeks after you have read the book, to renew the concepts and tools by applying them

- As often as desired to think through important influence opportunities (if you expect to use the workbook in this way, you may decide to use postable notes rather than writing in it.) Additional forms for many of the planning exercises are provided in the back of this workbook.

- As a journal for personal reflections about your own growth as an influencer and leader.

Throughout the workbook, we will refer to *Exercising Influence: A Guide for Making Things Happen at Work, at Home, and in Your Community* as "the book," to the handbook you are now reading as "the workbook," and to the seminar entitled *Exercising Influence: Building Relationships and Getting Results* as "the workshop." In addition, *Exercising Influence: A Discussion Guide for Team Leaders and Group Facilitators* will be of great value should you wish to have a conversation about the topic with a group or team.

The questions in the workbook are designed to achieve two purposes:

- To help you reflect on your "career" as an influencer and to provide some structure for further growth and development of your influence skills

- To assist you in preparing for specific influence opportunities.

In Part I and Part III, you will have an opportunity to reflect on your own attitudes toward and approach to influence and leadership. Part II is primarily ocused on the specifics of planning for a particular influence opportunity. For each 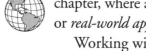 chapter, where appropriate, the exercises will be labeled either *personal reflection* or *real-world application.*

Working with a partner or a group committed to learning together and providing honest feedback to one another will enhance your learning experience immeasurably.

Once you have read the book, you may decide to use this workbook in a different order from the way it is presented here.

Exercising Influence

Self-Assessment

Before you begin using this workbook, we recommend that you take this brief self-assessment. After completing the instrument, transfer your scores to the graphic on page 5 and then review the description of the influence tactics in the book, Part I.

Influence Behavior: Self-Assessment

Rate yourself on the following behaviors. Think about how you influence others. This rating will provide valuable information to you in developing a mutually beneficial influence relationship with your colleagues. Use the symbols below to record your responses in the boxes to the right of the questions. When you have finished, transfer your symbols to the graphic on the next page, then look at the key that follows. This will give you an idea of the way you are currently influencing others.

N/A = Not applicable (Not appropriate or needed in the situations you face.)

⇧ = I could do this more often. (If I used this behavior more, I would exercise influence more effectively.)

✓ = I do this about as often as I would like. (I am satisfied with the frequency with which I use this behavior.)

⇩ = I could do this less often. (I feel that I use this behavior more frequently than is appropriate.)

★ = I do this differently from the way I would prefer. (I would like to do this differently and more effectively, regardless of frequency. For example, I may give reasons in the appropriate situations, but if I chose reasons that were more convincing to the other person, it would be more effective.)

You may find that you want to use more than one symbol. For example, you may think that you use a behavior less often than you want *and* that you want to do it differently. You would then mark "⇧" and "★" in the box.

1. Offer useful suggestions. ☐

2. Express needs directly. ☐

3. Support my proposals with good reasons. ☐

4. Show others how my proposal fits in with what they believe or hope to achieve. ☐

5. Willing to offer a fair exchange when asking something of others. ☐

6. Let others know of any realistic consequences to them in taking or not taking an action. ☐

7. Help others see a clear vision of success at the end of the road I would like them to take. ☐

8. Actively encourage others to take action. ☐

9. Ask thought-provoking questions. ☐

10. Explore information and ideas, don't just take things at face value. ☐

11. Paraphrase what others have said and check my understanding. ☐

(Continued)

Influence Behavior: Self-Assessment (continued)

12. Test the strength of another's position or concern by carrying it to its logical conclusion. ☐

13. Find and comment on areas of mutual concern or interest. ☐

14. Be open about my motivation. ☐

15. Help others to clarify issues that are facing them. ☐

16. Challenge others to come up with ideas for action steps they could take. ☐

Excerpted from Exercising Influence: Building Relationships and Getting Results, a copyrighted program of Barnes & Conti Associates, Inc., Berkeley, California. Used by permission.

Interpreting Your Self-Assessment

This instrument is not a formal test of your influence skills. It is an experience in self-observation and self-reflection. As such, it is a tool that can give you some useful guidance if you use it in an experimental and creative way. You have answered some questions about your use of influence skills in general. This will give you some insight into where to focus your influence skill study and practice. For example, if you find that your "up" (do more) arrows are concentrated in the Expressive tactics (Tell, Sell, Negotiate, Enlist), you might re-read Chapter 4 and follow the suggestions as to where those skills can be most useful. Create a list of opportunities to practice the skills, ask for feedback from someone you trust, and take time to reflect on the impact of your influence approach in each situation. If you gave yourself some "down" (do less) arrows on one or two tactics, create a plan for an upcoming situation that will require you to use different behaviors from your "default" approach.

You may also want to use this instrument to think about which of these skills you tend to use in a specific influence relationship. Then plan an influence opportunity with that person during which you will consciously use some different behaviors.

Another possible application is to use the instrument as the basis for a conversation with a coaching partner who has had the opportunity to observe you in a variety of situations and can give you specific feedback on how you currently use each of the behaviors and ideas for developing less effectively used behaviors.

Exercising Influence Framework: Results

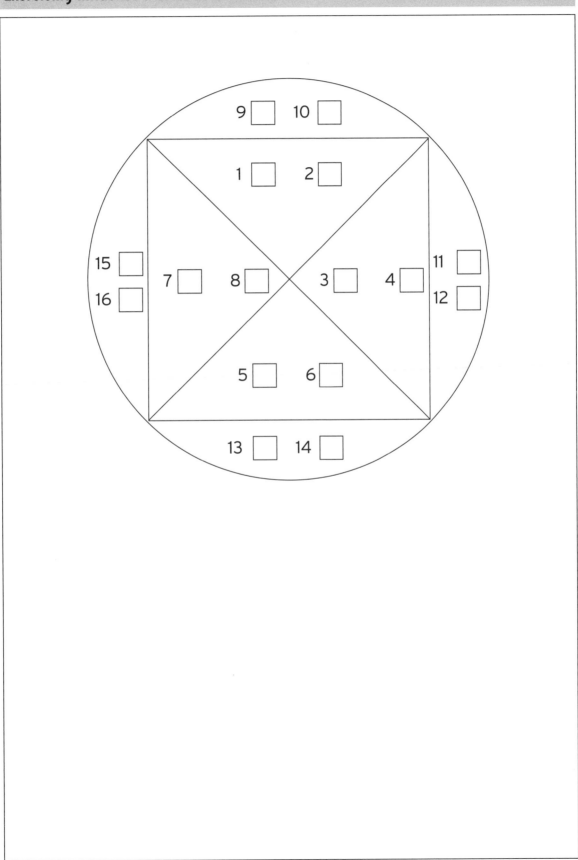

Exercising Influence Instrument: Results

Exercising Influence Model

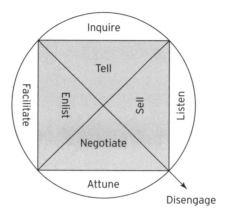

 Based on your self-assessment, answer the following questions:

Which of the tactics do you tend to overuse?

Which do you tend to underuse?

Which tactics would you like to use in a different and more effective way?

Which of the tactics, if used more effectively, will be most useful to you in your current roles? Future roles?

CHAPTER 1

What We've Got Here Is Failure to Influence. . .

IN THE FIRST CHAPTER of the *Exercising Influence* book, there are several examples of situations in which the subject needs the help, support, or resources of other people in order to accomplish a goal. Take a few minutes to reflect on goals that are currently important to you—goals that you believe will require the support, resources, commitment, or assistance of others. Some of them are probably associated with situations in your work life, some with your personal life, and perhaps you also have goals related to your community. These situations and your goals for them may be something you would like to start, develop, achieve, or change. List some of the most important ones on the following page.

Some things I'd like to accomplish at work:

-
-
-

Some things I'd like to accomplish in my personal life:

-
-
-

Some things I'd like to accomplish in one or more of the communities that I am part of:

-
-
-

CHAPTER 2

What Is Influence, and Why Do We Want to Have It?

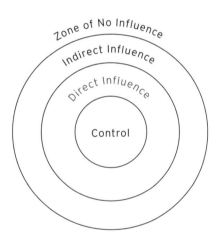

TAKE A FEW MINUTES to think about yourself as an influencer and leader. Fill out the Sphere of Influence graphic below; then answer the questions on the facing page. Refer to pages 12 through 15 in the book.

Sphere of Influence

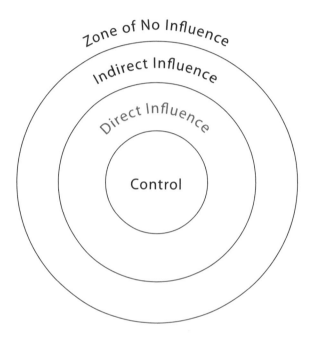

(Continued)

(Continued)

How satisfied are you with your current sphere of influence? What, if anything, would you like to change about it?

What are your primary sources of power? How do you use them? To what degree are you currently satisfied with the way you use power? What would you like to change?

Where do you now exercise leadership? Where do you have other opportunities to exercise leadership? To what degree are you now satisfied with the way you exercise leadership? What would you like to change?

(Continued)

What might stop you from taking opportunities to lead or influence others? What do you say to yourself that causes you to hold back? What might be the costs of exercising influence or leadership?

What do you see as the benefits of becoming a more effective influencer?

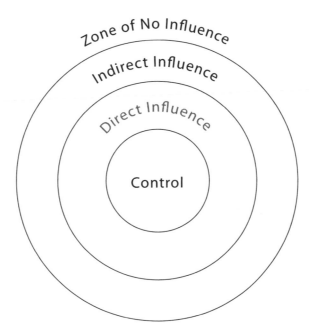 Think about the situations and goals you listed earlier. You can think of them as influence opportunities. It's possible that some of the goals you have in these situations can be accomplished by yourself or through the use of your legitimate power or authority. (For example, if you're the president of a community organization and want to call a meeting of the board, you may have the authority to do so. Of course, that doesn't necessarily mean that anyone else will show up.) Some of these opportunities may require the help of other people to whom you have direct access. Still others may depend on the support of persons or groups whom you can only influence indirectly. And there are probably some situations in which your success will depend greatly on conditions over which you have no control or influence.

Below is a graphic that represents your sphere of influence. Write three of the most important influence opportunities on separate small postable notes and place them below the graphic. Then answer the questions on the next pages, referring to the graphic as you identify the elements in your sphere of influence for each opportunity.

Zone of No Influence

Indirect Influence

Direct Influence

Control

(Continued)

(Continued)

Where do you have direct power (that is, you have the ability to make something happen directly that will help you achieve a goal)? What are the sources of your power?

Opportunity 1	Opportunity 2	Opportunity 3

Where do you have direct influence with others who can help you achieve your goals in each situation? Who is in your direct sphere of influence?

Opportunity 1	Opportunity 2	Opportunity 3

(Continued)

(Continued)

Where do you have indirect influence with those who can help you achieve your most important goals (that is, you can influence them through another person, through a group, through sending them a book or article, etc.)?

Opportunity 1	Opportunity 2	Opportunity 3

What elements that can have an impact on your ability to achieve your goals are in the zone where you have no power or influence?

Opportunity 1	Opportunity 2	Opportunity 3

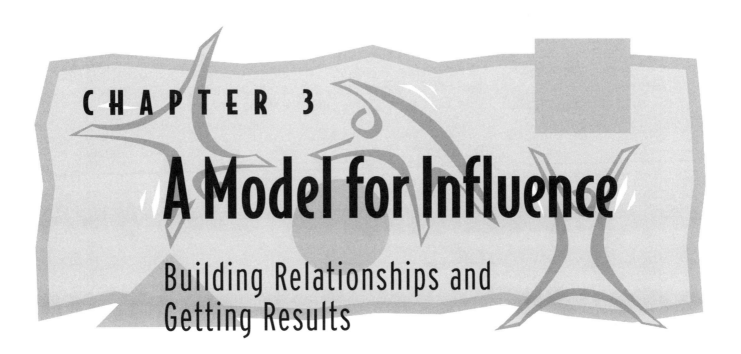

CHAPTER 3

A Model for Influence

Building Relationships and Getting Results

 REVIEW THE DISCUSSION of the Influence Framework on pages 21 and 22 in the book. Reflect on three recent influence opportunities. Use the formulation "Influence [person] to [action]." List them below.

Opportunity 1

Influence _____ to _____.

Opportunity 2

Influence _____ to _____.

Opportunity 3

Influence _____ to _____.

To what degree did you consider each aspect of the Influence Framework before entering the situation?

- Opportunity 1: _____

- Opportunity 2: _____

- Opportunity 3: _____

What patterns or habits are you aware of in the way you approach an influence opportunity based on this reflection?

Choose one of the situations you listed earlier that meets the following criteria:

- *Current*–this situation exists in the present; you have an opportunity to achieve a goal in the foreseeable future.

- *Important*–achieving the goal will make a significant and positive difference to you.

- *Ambitious*–it will require some real effort to achieve your goal in this situation.

- *Requires direct influence*–this is not something you can do by yourself, nor is it dependent on people you have no access to.

You will use this situation, focusing on one important influence relationship, to apply the ideas and tools in the *Exercising Influence* book. Describe the situation briefly below or transfer your postable note from the previous exercise.

Situation

Identify a person who is important to the success of this goal and with whom you have direct influence (that is, you have ready access to the person). Identify the person and say why he or she is important to your achievement of this goal.

Influence Target

(Continued)

Consider the discussion of the Influence Framework in Chapter 3 of the book. Thinking about the situation and the person you identified, answer the questions below, then place key words in the appropriate spaces on the Influence Framework. This is Part 1 of the Planning Guide, and the first page can also be used as a quick reference sheet for this situation.

What would success look like overall? Specifically, what **results** do you want to accomplish with this person?

How would you describe your influence **relationship** with this person now? Is there any-thing from the past that would either help or hinder you in influencing him or her? What kind of influence relationship do you hope to have with him or her in the future?

How do you usually go about influencing this person? What is your **approach?** If you had to influence him or her about this today, which tactics would you be likely to use? (Refer to the chart on page 27 in Chapter 3 of the book.) Later you will return to this chart after deciding on the most useful tactics and behaviors.

What is the background or **context** for this influence opportunity? What is going on that might have an impact on your success:

- For the individual

- In the organization

- Related to the culture (national, ethnic, industry, organizational, departmental, or professional)

Are there one or more **issues** involved that will lend themselves to the study and explo-ration of information and different points of view? If so, what are they?

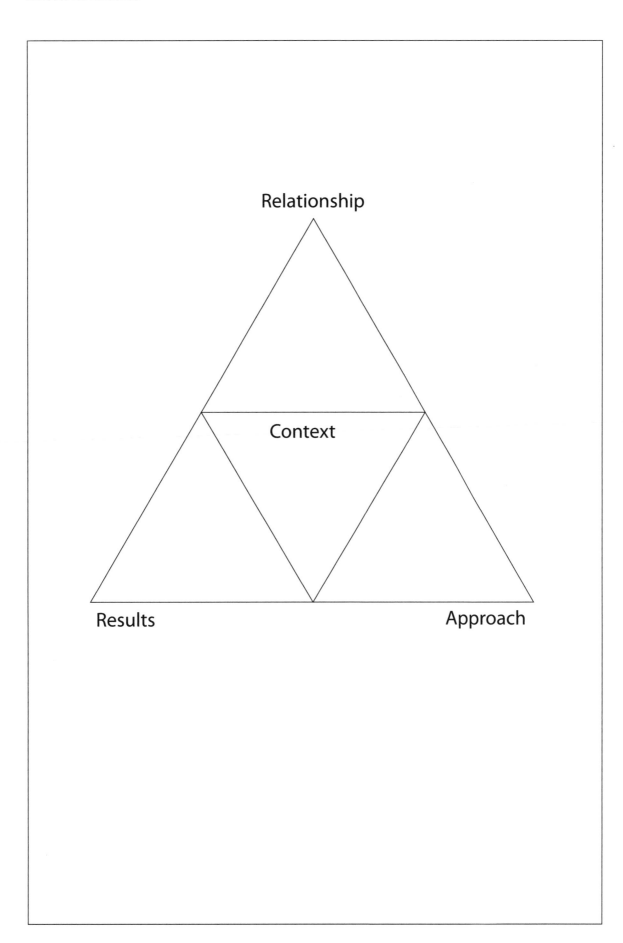

Influence Framework Reference Sheet

Situation:

Influence Target:

My Sphere of Influence Related to This Opportunity

Zone of No Influence

Indirect Influence

Direct Influence

Control

CHAPTER 4

Expressive Influence

Sending Ideas and Generating Energy

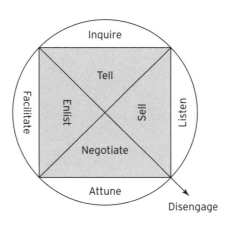

In general:

Where could you use Expressive behaviors more often or more effectively?

- At work

- At home

- In your community

Which of the Expressive behaviors would you most like to develop?

What are your hopes and fears regarding the use of Expressive influence?

- Results I believe I could improve or achieve through the more effective use of Expressive influence:

- Results, reactions, or responses that I would NOT want to happen as a result of using Expressive influence:

Identify a good partner with whom you could practice using Expressive influence, someone you trust to give you honest feedback about the impact of your behavior.

Now consider the influence situation you have selected.

Select two of the Expressive influence tactics that you believe would be most useful to you in this situation. Think about why you would want to use them and what results you hope to achieve by doing so (for example, "Enlist: to create some enthusiasm for the new project"). Make notes in the text boxes below each of the tactics.

Expressive Tactic 1: _____

Expressive Tactic 2: _____

CHAPTER 5

Receptive Influence

Inviting Ideas and Stimulating Action

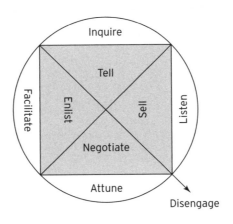

In general:

Where could you use Receptive behaviors more often or more effectively?

- At work

- At home

- In your community

Which of the Receptive behaviors would you most like to develop?

What are your hopes and fears regarding the use of Receptive influence?

- Results I believe I could improve or achieve through the more effective use of Receptive influence:

- Results, reactions, or responses that I would NOT want to happen as a result of using Receptive influence:

Identify a good partner with whom you could practice using Receptive influence, someone you trust to give you honest feedback about the impact of your behavior.

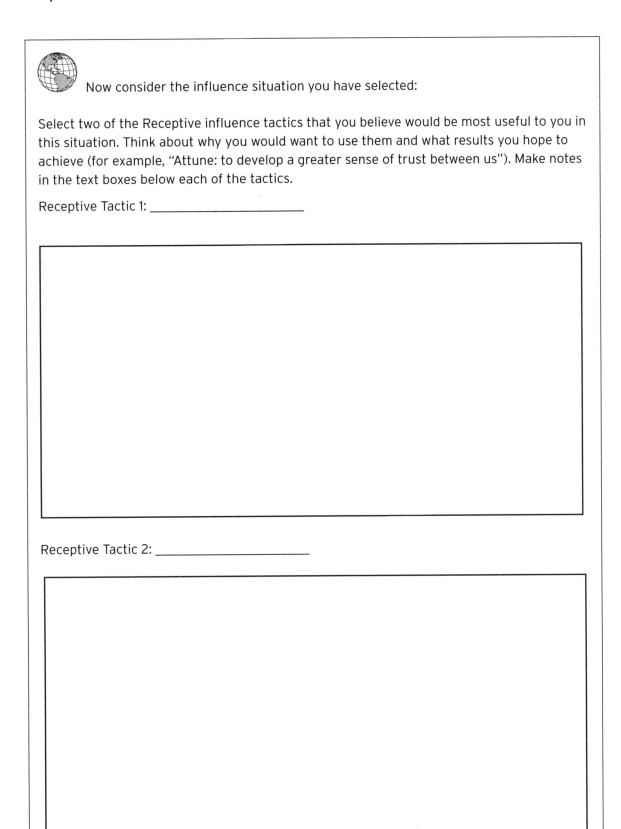

Now consider the influence situation you have selected:

Select two of the Receptive influence tactics that you believe would be most useful to you in this situation. Think about why you would want to use them and what results you hope to achieve (for example, "Attune: to develop a greater sense of trust between us"). Make notes in the text boxes below each of the tactics.

Receptive Tactic 1: _____

Receptive Tactic 2: _____

When you are clear about the Receptive tactics that would be most useful in this situation, write them in the Influence Framework on page 22 of this workbook.

CHAPTER 6

Influencing in Action

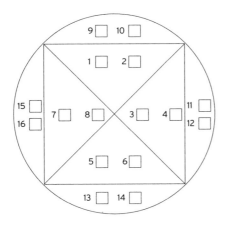

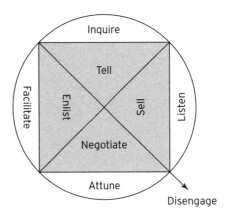

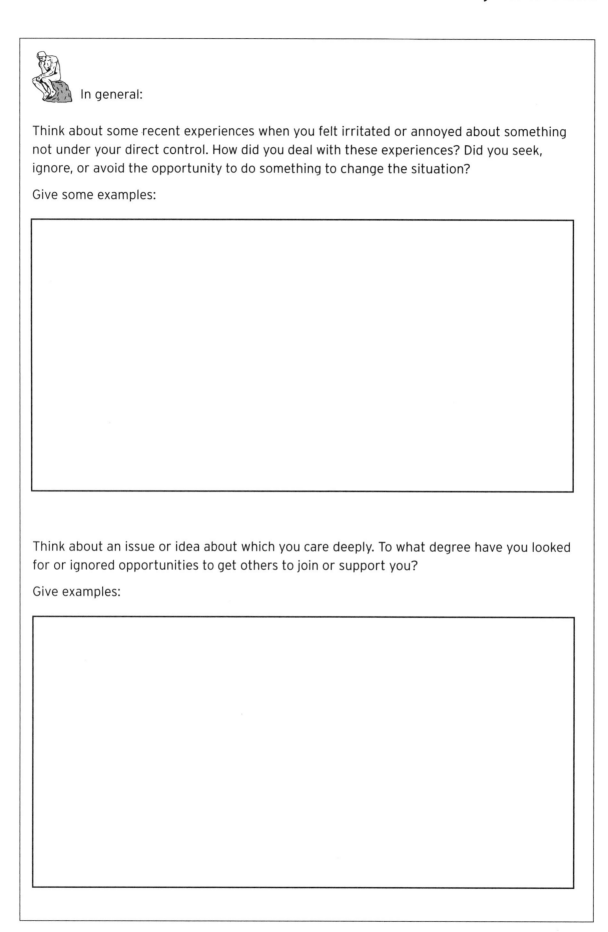

In general:

Think about some recent experiences when you felt irritated or annoyed about something not under your direct control. How did you deal with these experiences? Did you seek, ignore, or avoid the opportunity to do something to change the situation?

Give some examples:

Think about an issue or idea about which you care deeply. To what degree have you looked for or ignored opportunities to get others to join or support you?

Give examples:

Think about some recent times when you wanted or needed something from others. To what degree did you take actions with the purpose of meeting your needs?

Give examples:

What influence opportunities could you create right now to deal with any of these situations?

Give examples:

PART II

Planning for Influence

CHAPTER 7

Developing an Influence Plan

Potential Costs of Active Influencing	Potential Benefits of Active Influencing

To begin this phase of your self-study or application, reflect on your selected influence opportunity. List below the costs and the benefits of making a serious effort to influence the other person consciously and actively. Write down everything that comes to mind without self-editing.

Influence Opportunity: _____

Potential Costs of Active Influencing	Potential Benefits of Active Influencing

(Continued)

(Continued)

If you think this opportunity is important enough to risk the potential costs in time, energy, resources, lost opportunities, or other possibilities in order to gain the benefits, you can move forward with influence planning. If, on reflection, the costs seem too high or the benefits too small to justify the effort, go back and choose a different situation to focus on.

Chapters 8 through 15 in this workbook will take you step-by-step through the planning process for the situation you have selected. There are additional copies of the Planning Guide at the end of the workbook.

CHAPTER 8

Establishing Influence Goals

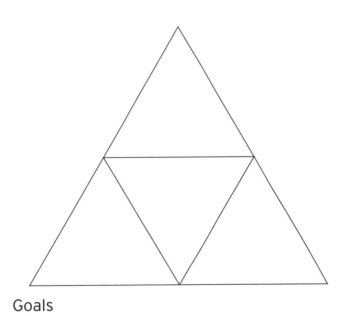

Goals

In this chapter and Chapters 9 through 11, you will find a series of questions that fall within each of the areas of the Influence Framework. Review the questions in each area and highlight the ones that you believe to be relevant to the outcome of your influence opportunity. Answer those key questions, then think how you will use the information to build the influence relationship, and achieve your desired results.

Begin by focusing on the results you would like to achieve.

Results

- What is your vision of success? What role will the other person play in it?

- What are the needs that underlie your vision? For you? For the organization? For the person you are influencing?

- What specific long-term and short-term goals do you have for the influence opportunity?

- What are your criteria for success? How will you know you have achieved the results you are aiming for?

- What alternative outcomes might satisfy the underlying needs and achieve equivalent results?

(Continued)

(Continued)

Based on your exploration, rewrite or highlight your most important influence goal in this situation, using the FOCUS criteria to sharpen it.

Criteria for Influence Goals	Goal:
• Flexible • Observable • Courageous • Useful • Supportive	

When you have answered the questions, note the most relevant points on your Influence Framework Reference Sheet at the end of the workbook for this situation. Consider how willing you are to be persistent in attaining your goal.

CHAPTER 9

Focus on the Relationship

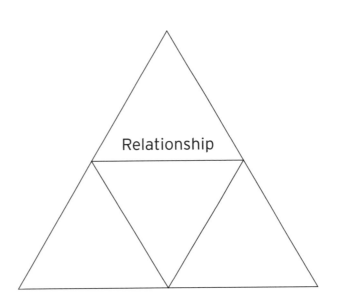

Continue your analysis of the situation by examining the influence relationship you have with the other person.

Relationship

- What is the history of your (or your team's) influence relationship (in both directions) with this person or group?

- What is the current level of trust? Why?

- What assumptions do each of you hold about the other? How will you test them? How might they affect the outcome?

- What is the power balance between you? Who needs whom the most?

- What are the current or continuing issues in the relationship, regardless of whether they are directly related to this influence opportunity?

(Continued)

Consider whether, given the current state of the relationship, this person is ready to be influenced by you. If not, how might you apply some of the ideas from Chapter 9 in the book to start, develop, change, improve, or salvage this influence relationship before you get down to the business you have in mind?

When you have answered the questions, note the most relevant points on your Influence Framework Reference Sheet for this situation. Consider how willing you are to be active in developing this influence relationship.

CHAPTER 10

Focus on the Context

The Individual

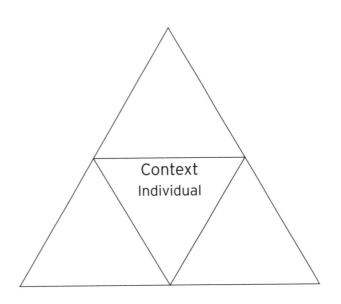

Context

Individual

Develop information about the other person and yourself.

Context

What are the relevant values of the other person? How are they similar or different from yours?

Other:

You:

What are his or her high priority goals right now? Yours?

Other:

You:

What common or conflicting vested interests are important in this situation? What do each of you have to gain or lose?

Other:

You:

(Continued)

(Continued)

What are the important current issues that have an impact on this person? How might your influence goal be related to these issues?

Issues for the other:

Relevance to influence goal:

How would you describe his or her communication or work style? How does he or she generally prefer to be approached? How does your usual approach match with his or her preferences? How might you want to modify it?

Other's preferences:

Your approach:

As you review what you have written, be alert for signs of your own assumptions. Consider whether there might be alternate explanations for some of this person's actions.

When you have answered the questions, note the most relevant points on your Influence Framework Reference Sheet for this situation. Consider how willing you are to reexamine some of your assumptions about the other person.

CHAPTER 11

Focus on the Context

System, Organization, Culture, Timing

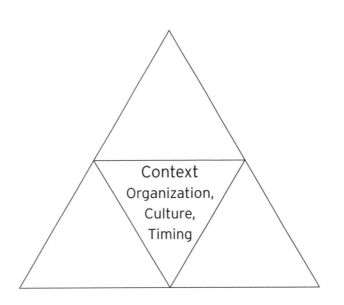

Context
Organization,
Culture,
Timing

Now think about the system that surrounds the person you are planning to influence. In particular, note organizational and cultural factors that can help or hinder you in achieving results.

Organizational

How does the strategy of the organization (or the way the family sees its future) relate to the subject at hand? Are the results you envision a good "fit" for the organizational strategy and goals?

How will the organization's (or family's) structure, processes, and/or politics affect your influence approach? Is your preferred approach out of the norm?

Where do issues relevant to your influence goal stand in the ranking of organizational or family priorities?

How might the formal or informal power structure in the organization or family affect the outcome of your influence opportunity?

Who are other stakeholders in the outcome of your action? How will you involve them?

(Continued)

(Continued)

Cultural

What are the cultural values (organizational, professional, national, or ethnic) that are relevant to this issue? (For example, might the other be so committed to his or her interpretation of the value of "respecting people" that he or she might not be willing to consider changing the organization if it would require some cuts in staff?)

What are the norms (formal or informal ground rules) that you should be aware of? (For example, should you always send an agenda ahead of a meeting? Is there a family norm not to talk about contentious issues at the dinner table?)

What are some of the cultural assumptions that relate to this situation? (For example, might the other assume that you have no financial acumen because you work in HR? Might your spouse think your opinion is not informed on a particular topic because of your gender?)

What are the usual cultural practices or rituals that might be useful in this situation? (For example, does a "business lunch" in a quiet setting create a better atmosphere for influence or do stand-up meetings with get-to-the-point agendas work better?)

Are there any cultural taboos that could derail your approach? (For example, are there any unwritten rules against approaching a senior executive directly without informing your boss? Do your elderly parents come from a culture in which they expect their children to take their advice rather than vice-versa?)

(Continued)

(Continued)

External Trends and Issues

What is going on right now in the larger systems of which you and the person you are influencing are a part that could have an impact on your influence opportunity? Consider some of the factors you listed earlier as being outside your sphere of control or influence.

After reviewing your thoughts on the system, highlight key points that you will want to take into consideration and adjust for. What does the context you have examined so far suggest about the timing of your approach?

When you have answered the questions, note the most relevant points on your Influence Framework Reference Sheet for this situation. Consider how the system will affect the outcome of your influence opportunity and how you will need to work with or around it.

CHAPTER 12

Focus on the Context

Yourself

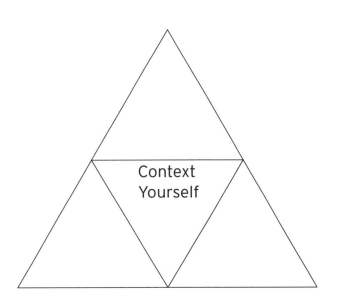

Context
Yourself

You've looked at individual context as well as elements of the surrounding systems that will be important to your success. Now it's time to take a deeper look at yourself as an influencer.

Refer to the self-assessment (page 1) you did at the beginning of this self-study process. Then reflect on what has made you successful as an influencer so far. What types of influence situations are easiest for you to handle? What do you currently see as your strengths (characteristics, knowledge, and skills) that have been critical to your success? List them below.

Now consider what you find most challenging and difficult about influence. What characteristics, skills, knowledge, or the lack thereof, have come in the way of your success from time to time? What types of influence situations are least comfortable for you? What do you see as your most important limitations or areas for improvement?

Identify one or more people whom you trust and with whom you have a reasonably good influence relationship. Ask the person to give you feedback about your influence skills. What works well, and what doesn't work as well? Some questions that might be useful would be:

- In what ways am I most effective when I try to influence you?

- In what ways do you see me being effective in influencing others?

- What do I do when I am trying to influence you that is ineffective?

(Continued)

- What do you observe me doing ineffectively when I am trying to influence other people?

- What suggestions do you have that would help me be more effective as an influencer with you or others?

After the conversations, write down key elements of the feedback in the two columns below.

Feedback That Confirms the Way I See Myself	Feedback That Is Surprising or Disconfirming

(Continued)

Disconfirming feedback may be either positive or negative. It's just different from the way you have seen yourself and offers you information on what could be "blind spots" in your influence approach.

If you find that some of the feedback helps you see where you might go off-track without realizing it, you will want to take some action to be more aware of it. If you find that you do something naturally that works well for certain people, you might want to do it more consciously and frequently.

 Now consider how your strengths, limitations, and blind spots might play out in this specific situation.

One blind spot that can be especially challenging to confront is one's own motivation for influencing. Clarity about this is essential to success. Revisit the goal(s) you identified earlier. Ask yourself: "What would achieving this goal do for me?" and record your responses below.

If you find that one of these responses is a better representation of your influence goal, add it to your Reference Sheet for this situation and review the rest of the information in light of that insight.

How can you use your strengths to best effect in this situation? (For example, if you are at your best in informal settings and it is appropriate to the situation and the other's preferences, raise the issue over lunch or during a social or athletic activity. If you are very comfortable with expressing your needs directly and Tell is one of the tactics you plan to use, choose that as the specific behavior, as long as it doesn't conflict with organizational or cultural norms.)

How might your limitations, especially if they are blind spots, affect your results? What will you do to minimize their impact? (For example, you might rehearse the situation with a partner who will give you honest feedback about your tendency to mumble or meander when you engage around difficult issues.)

CHAPTER 13

Focus on the Issues

You've looked at the conditions that are relevant to your influence opportunity. Now it's time to engage more deeply with the issues. An issue is a central or very important topic in a discussion—one that is of concern to the participants. A request for action always raises issues of concern.

What are the primary issues that will be raised in association with your influence goal (especially from the other person's point of view)? Highlight the ones that are the most important, difficult, or challenging for you to respond to. (Many issues are articulated as "What about. . . ?")

•

•

•

•

Choose one of the issues highlighted above; gather the best (most objective and reliable) information you can; then articulate your own position or opinion. Use the table on the next page to record key points.

(Continued)

Issue:

Your position:

Arguments That Support Your Position	Arguments Against Your Position	Potential Costs to the Other	Potential Benefits to the Other	Vested Interests and Needs Involved	Examples and Benchmarks

(Continued)

Highlight the most relevant points (those that will have the most importance to the other person). This will be especially useful for you in thinking through how you will use Expressive influence. Quality and relevance are keys to success with Expressive behavior. Remember that Receptive behaviors are likely to be very useful in drawing information and ideas about the issue from others, including the person you are influencing.

CHAPTER 14

Choosing and Using Influence Behaviors to Achieve Your Goal

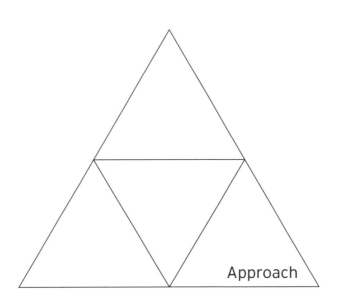

Approach

You are now in a position to select the best and most useful behaviors to achieve your influence goal.

Select the specific behaviors that you expect to be your most useful tools in the situation.

Behaviors

- Given your analysis of the situation, what do you intend your influence behaviors to achieve? Review the tactics that you chose earlier and modify as needed. Two Expressive and two Receptive tactics are generally enough to plan for. Edit your Influence Framework Reference Sheet as appropriate.

- What are the best specific behaviors to achieve those results? Refer to pages 97 and 98 in the book for guidance. When you have selected the behaviors, add them to the Reference Sheet.

Now complete Part 2 of the Planning Guide.

(Continued)

(Continued)

Planning Guide: Part 2

Considering all of the information you developed in Part 1 of the Planning Guide, develop your plan.

- Write down a few ideas about how you plan to use the behaviors. Refer to the sentence starters in Appendix D of the book for suggestions.

- Plan a sequence (be aware that the other person will be actively influencing you as well, so you may have to change your plan "on the fly.") Which of the tactics and specific behaviors will you begin with? Which ones will be most useful to you toward the conclusion?

- Troubleshoot. Think about how the conversation could go wrong and what you will do about it if that should happen. (For example, "If the other person becomes angry or upset, then I will switch to Listening behaviors.")

    If . . .

    If . . .

    If . . .

- Focus on your next steps. What will you do if you achieve your goal? What will you do if you don't?

(Continued)

Set yourself up for success. For ideas, refer to Chapter 14, page 100 in the book.

- What actions might you want to take before you meet with the other in order to create the conditions for success?

- What actions will you take early in the meeting, before you get down to business, that will create a positive climate for influence?

- What actions will you take at the end of the meeting to make sure that you and the other person are "on the same page" about the results and that any agreements between you will be implemented?

CHAPTER 15

Putting Your Plan to Work

After the influence situation you planned for has taken place, ask yourself the following questions:

What worked well in the way I approached and handled the situation? What helped move us toward achieving my influence goal or acceptable alternative?

What was not effective in the way I approached and handled the situation? What made it difficult for us to achieve my goal or an acceptable alternative?

What was surprising to me during the actual situation? To what degree might I have anticipated that? How well did I handle it and how could I have handled it even better?

(Continued)

(Continued)

To what degree do I believe that the other person is satisfied with the outcome? How do I know this? What implementation issues may arise?

How might I have planned better for this situation?

What have I learned from this situation that I can apply to future influence opportunities?

What are some next steps to take with this person or around this issue with others?

PART III

Special Issues in Influence

CHAPTER 16

The Ethics of Influence

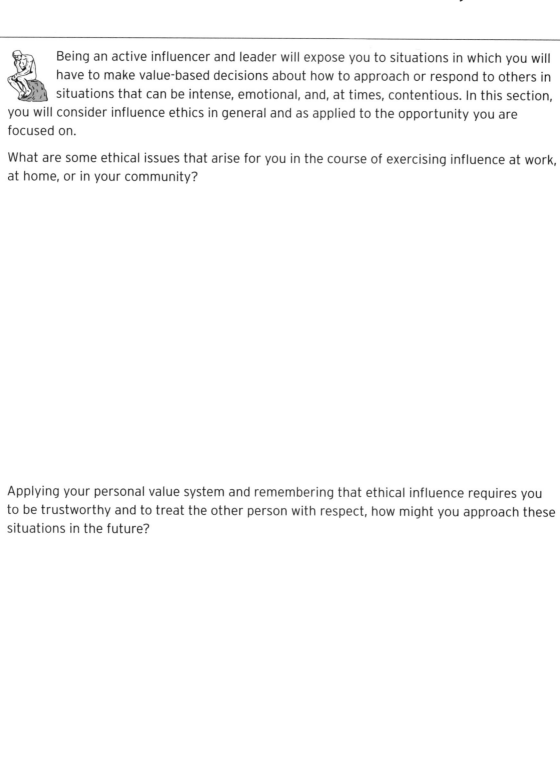 Being an active influencer and leader will expose you to situations in which you will have to make value-based decisions about how to approach or respond to others in situations that can be intense, emotional, and, at times, contentious. In this section, you will consider influence ethics in general and as applied to the opportunity you are focused on.

What are some ethical issues that arise for you in the course of exercising influence at work, at home, or in your community?

Applying your personal value system and remembering that ethical influence requires you to be trustworthy and to treat the other person with respect, how might you approach these situations in the future?

(Continued)

(Continued)

Now apply the same criteria to the influence opportunity you are focusing on.

What kinds of ethical issues could arise in relation to the influence opportunity you are planning for? How will you handle them?

CHAPTER 17

Influencing Electronically

Although e-mail, teleconferences, and instant messaging are not usually the ideal tools for interpersonal influence, there are times when we have no other options. Spend a few minutes reflecting on your own use of electronic media to influence.

Under what circumstances do you use electronic communication media to influence others? Is it possible to use other means in any of these situations? If so, what stops you from doing so?

What works best? (Consider what works best for you when you are on the receiving end as well as what seems to obtain the best results when you are the influencer.) Are there some influence situations or aspects of an influence approach in which electronic media are especially useful or effective for you?

How has using electronic means to influence been ineffective? What has not worked well? (Consider both your own influence results and your reaction to other people's attempts to influence you electronically.)

What will you do differently in the future to improve your chances of success?

(Continued)

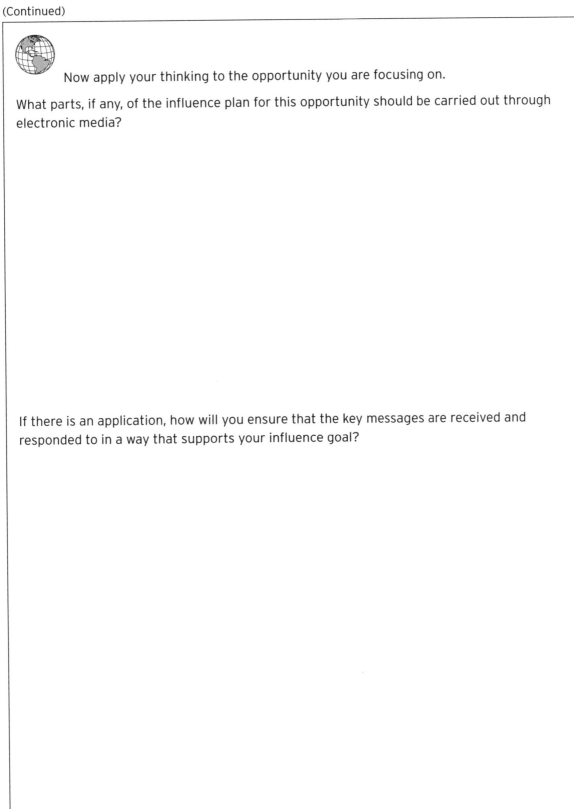

Now apply your thinking to the opportunity you are focusing on.

What parts, if any, of the influence plan for this opportunity should be carried out through electronic media?

If there is an application, how will you ensure that the key messages are received and responded to in a way that supports your influence goal?

CHAPTER 18

Influencing Indirectly

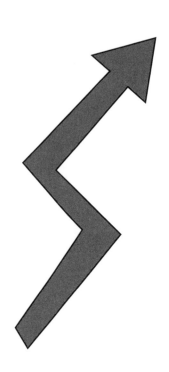

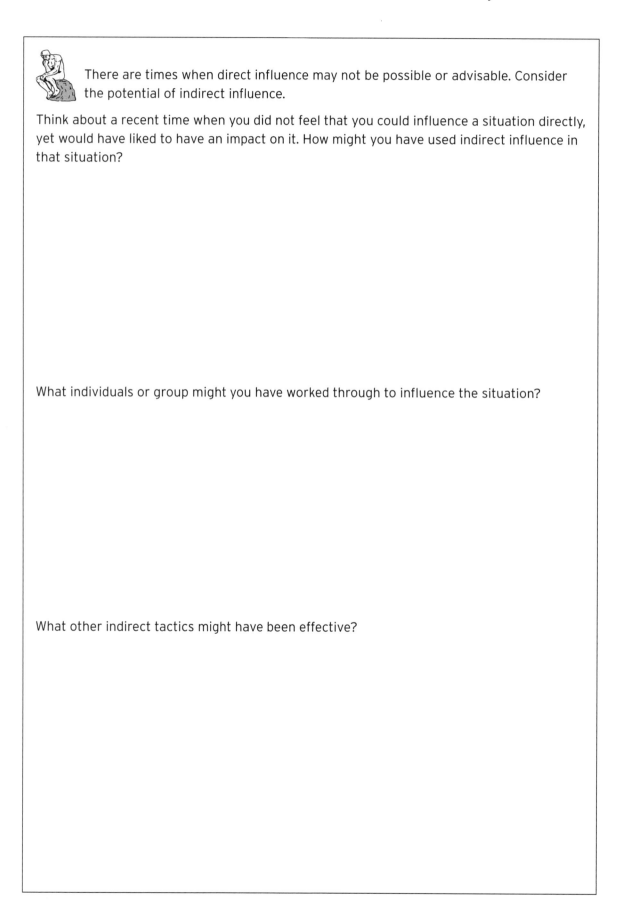

There are times when direct influence may not be possible or advisable. Consider the potential of indirect influence.

Think about a recent time when you did not feel that you could influence a situation directly, yet would have liked to have an impact on it. How might you have used indirect influence in that situation?

What individuals or group might you have worked through to influence the situation?

What other indirect tactics might have been effective?

(Continued)

 Now consider the potential of indirect influence for the opportunity you have chosen to focus on.

In addition to the direct tactics and behaviors you plan to use, how might you use indirect influence tactics to help you achieve your influence goal?

CHAPTER 19

Applied Influence

Making Things Happen

 BECOMING A MORE EFFECTIVE INFLUENCER and a more influential leader is a lifelong learning process. Now that you have read the book and worked your way through an application, you have some important tools for continuous learning. This is a conscious process and requires that you make some commitments to yourself.

How do you plan to continue developing your skills as an influencer?

In the next few weeks, where will you consciously put your influence "muscles" to work?

- At work

- At home

- In your community

Planning Guide: Preparation

Situation:

Influence Target:

Sphere of Influence

Situation:

Influence Target:

My Sphere of Influence Related to This Opportunity

Zone of No Influence

Indirect Influence

Direct Influence

Control

Planning Guide: Preparation (continued)

Costs and Benefits

Potential Costs of Active Influencing	Potential Benefits of Active Influencing

(Continued)

Planning Guide: Preparation (continued)

Issues

Issue 1:

Your position:

Arguments That Support Your Position	Arguments Against Your Position	Potential Costs to the Other	Potential Benefits to the Other	Vested Interests and Needs Involved	Examples and Benchmarks

(Continued)

Planning Guide: Preparation (continued)

Issues

Issue 2:

Your position:

Arguments That Support Your Position	Arguments Against Your Position	Potential Costs to the Other	Potential Benefits to the Other	Vested Interests and Needs Involved	Examples and Benchmarks

Planning Guide: Preparation (continued)

Issues

Issue 3:

Your position:

Arguments That Support Your Position	Arguments Against Your Position	Potential Costs to the Other	Potential Benefits to the Other	Vested Interests and Needs Involved	Examples and Benchmarks

Planning Guide: Part 1

Influence Framework Reference Sheet

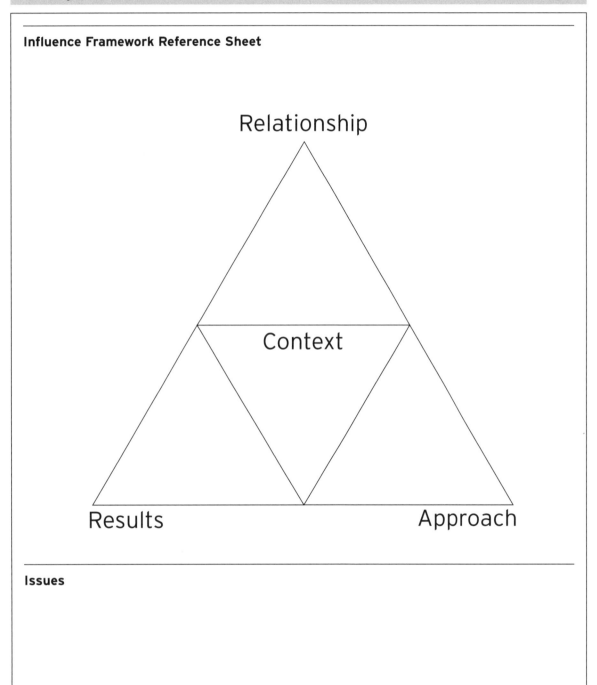

Issues

Planning Guide: Part 1 (continued)

What would success look like overall? Specifically, what results do you want to accomplish with this person?

How would you describe your influence relationship with this person now? Is there anything from the past that would either help or hinder you in influencing him or her? What kind of influence relationship do you hope to have with him or her in the future?

How do you usually go about influencing this person? If you had to influence him or her about this today, which tactics would you be likely to use? (Refer to the chart on page 27 in Chapter 3 of the book.) Later you will return to this chart after deciding on the most useful tactics and behaviors.

(Continued)

Planning Guide: Part 1 (continued)

What is the background or context for this influence opportunity? What is going on that might have an impact on your success:

- For the individual

- In the organization

- Related to the culture (national, ethnic, industry, organizational, departmental, or professional)

Are there one or more issues involved that will lend themselves to the study and exploration of information and different points of view? If so, what are they?

Planning Guide: Part 2

Considering all of the information you developed in Part 1 of the Planning Guide, develop your plan below.

- Write down a few ideas about how you plan to use the behaviors. Refer to the sentence starters in Appendix D of the book for suggestions. Consider whether and how to use electronic media (e-mail, teleconferences, web meetings, and so forth).

- Plan a sequence. (Be aware that the other person will be actively influencing you as well, so you may have to change your plan "on the fly.") Which of the tactics and specific behaviors will you begin with? Which ones will be most useful to you toward the conclusion?

- Troubleshoot. Think about how the conversation could go wrong and what you will do about it if that should happen, for example, "If the other person becomes angry or upset, then I will switch to Listening behaviors."

    If . . .

    If . . .

    If . . .

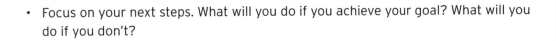

Planning Guide: Part 2 (continued)

- Focus on your next steps. What will you do if you achieve your goal? What will you do if you don't?

Set yourself up for success. For ideas, refer to page 100 in the book.

- What actions might you want to take before you meet with the other in order to create the conditions for success?

- What actions will you take at the end of the meeting to make sure that you and the other person are "on the same page" about the results and that any agreements between you will be implemented?

Planning Guide: Part 3

After the influence situation you planned for has taken place, ask yourself the following questions:

1. What worked well in the way I approached and handled the situation? What helped move us toward achieving my influence goal or acceptable alternative?

2. What was not effective in the way I approached and handled the situation? What made it difficult for us to achieve my goal or an acceptable alternative?

3. What was surprising to me during the actual situation? To what degree might I have anticipated that? How well did I handle it and how could I have handled it even better?

4. To what degree do I believe that the other person is satisfied with the outcome? How do I know this? What implementation issues may arise?

5. How might I have planned better for this situation?

6. What have I learned from this situation that I can apply to future influence opportunities?

7. What are some next steps to take with this person or around this issue with others?

Planning Guide: Preparation

Situation:

Influence Target:

Sphere of Influence

Situation:

Influence Target:

My Sphere of Influence Related to This Opportunity

Zone of No Influence

Indirect Influence

Direct Influence

Control

(Continued)

Planning Guide: Preparation (continued)

Costs and Benefits

Potential Costs of Active Influencing	Potential Benefits of Active Influencing

(Continued)

Planning Guide: Preparation (continued)

Issues

Issue 1:

Your position:

Arguments That Support Your Position	Arguments Against Your Position	Potential Costs to the Other	Potential Benefits to the Other	Vested Interests and Needs Involved	Examples and Benchmarks

(Continued)

Planning Guide: Preparation (continued)

Issues

Issue 2:

Your position:

Arguments That Support Your Position	Arguments Against Your Position	Potential Costs to the Other	Potential Benefits to the Other	Vested Interests and Needs Involved	Examples and Benchmarks

(Continued)

Planning Guide: Preparation (continued)

Issues

Issue 3:

Your position:

Arguments That Support Your Position	Arguments Against Your Position	Potential Costs to the Other	Potential Benefits to the Other	Vested Interests and Needs Involved	Examples and Benchmarks

Planning Guide: Part 1

Influence Framework Reference Sheet

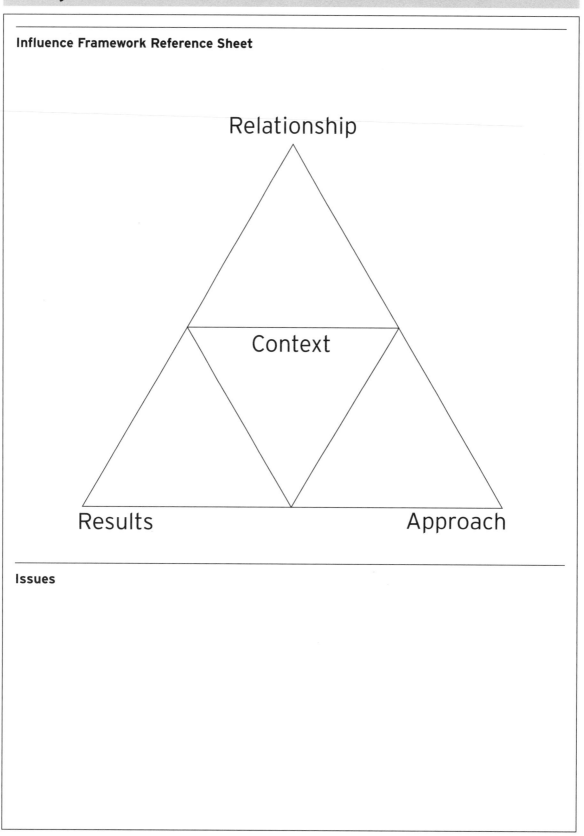

Issues

Planning Guide: Part 1 (continued)

What would success look like overall? Specifically, what results do you want to accomplish with this person?

How would you describe your influence relationship with this person now? Is there anything from the past that would either help or hinder you in influencing him or her? What kind of influence relationship do you hope to have with him or her in the future?

How do you usually go about influencing this person? If you had to influence him or her about this today, which tactics would you be likely to use? (Refer to the chart on page 27 in Chapter 3 of the book.) Later you will return to this chart after deciding on the most useful tactics and behaviors.

Planning Guide: Part 1 (continued)

What is the background or context for this influence opportunity? What is going on that might have an impact on your success:

- For the individual

- In the organization

- Related to the culture (national, ethnic, industry, organizational, departmental, or professional)

Are there one or more issues involved that will lend themselves to the study and exploration of information and different points of view? If so, what are they?

Planning Guide: Part 2

Considering all of the information you developed in Part 1 of the Planning Guide, develop your plan below.

- Write down a few ideas about how you plan to use the behaviors. Refer to the sentence starters in Appendix D of the book for suggestions. Consider whether and how to use electronic media (e-mail, teleconferences, web meetings, and so forth).

- Plan a sequence. (Be aware that the other person will be actively influencing you as well, so you may have to change your plan "on the fly.") Which of the tactics and specific behaviors will you begin with? Which ones will be most useful to you toward the conclusion?

- Troubleshoot. Think about how the conversation could go wrong and what you will do about it if that should happen, for example, "If the other person becomes angry or upset, then I will switch to Listening behaviors."

    If . . .

    If . . .

    If . . .

Planning Guide: Part 2 (continued)

- Focus on your next steps. What will you do if you achieve your goal? What will you do if you don't?

Set yourself up for success. For ideas, refer to page 100 in the book.

- What actions might you want to take before you meet with the other in order to create the conditions for success?

- What actions will you take at the end of the meeting to make sure that you and the other person are "on the same page" about the results and that any agreements between you will be implemented?

Planning Guide: Part 3

After the influence situation you planned for has taken place, ask yourself the following questions:

1. What worked well in the way I approached and handled the situation? What helped move us toward achieving my influence goal or acceptable alternative?

2. What was not effective in the way I approached and handled the situation? What made it difficult for us to achieve my goal or an acceptable alternative?

3. What was surprising to me during the actual situation? To what degree might I have anticipated that? How well did I handle it and how could I have handled it even better?

4. To what degree do I believe that the other person is satisfied with the outcome? How do I know this? What implementation issues may arise?

5. How might I have planned better for this situation?

6. What have I learned from this situation that I can apply to future influence opportunities?

7. What are some next steps to take with this person or around this issue with others?

Planning Guide: Preparation

Situation:

Influence Target:

Sphere of Influence

Situation:

Influence Target:

My Sphere of Influence Related to This Opportunity

Zone of No Influence

Indirect Influence

Direct Influence

Control

Planning Guide: Preparation (continued)

Costs and Benefits

Potential Costs of Active Influencing	Potential Benefits of Active Influencing

Planning Guide: Preparation (continued)

Issues

Issue 1:

Your position:

Arguments That Support Your Position	Arguments Against Your Position	Potential Costs to the Other	Potential Benefits to the Other	Vested Interests and Needs Involved	Examples and Benchmarks

Planning Guide: Preparation (continued)

Issues

Issue 2:

Your position:

Arguments That Support Your Position	Arguments Against Your Position	Potential Costs to the Other	Potential Benefits to the Other	Vested Interests and Needs Involved	Examples and Benchmarks

Planning Guide: Preparation (continued)

Issues

Issue 3:

Your position:

Arguments That Support Your Position	Arguments Against Your Position	Potential Costs to the Other	Potential Benefits to the Other	Vested Interests and Needs Involved	Examples and Benchmarks

Planning Guide: Part 1

Influence Framework Reference Sheet

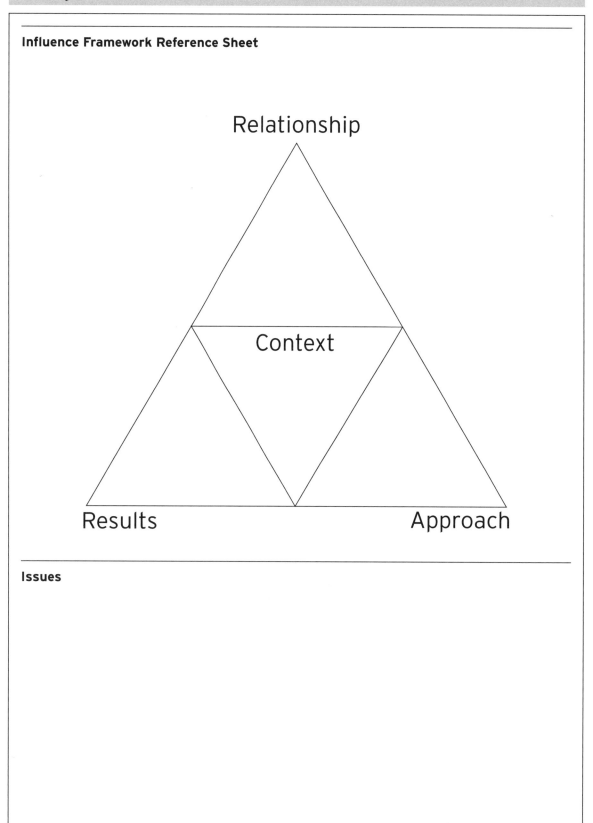

Issues

Planning Guide: Part 1 (continued)

What would success look like overall? Specifically, what results do you want to accomplish with this person?

How would you describe your influence relationship with this person now? Is there anything from the past that would either help or hinder you in influencing him or her? What kind of influence relationship do you hope to have with him or her in the future?

How do you usually go about influencing this person? If you had to influence him or her about this today, which tactics would you be likely to use? (Refer to the chart on page 27 in Chapter 3 of the book.) Later you will return to this chart after deciding on the most useful tactics and behaviors.

(Continued)

Planning Guide: Part 1 (continued)

What is the background or context for this influence opportunity? What is going on that might have an impact on your success:

- For the individual

- In the organization

- Related to the culture (national, ethnic, industry, organizational, departmental, or professional)

Are there one or more issues involved that will lend themselves to the study and exploration of information and different points of view? If so, what are they?

Planning Guide: Part 2

Considering all of the information you developed in Part 1 of the Planning Guide, develop your plan below.

- Write down a few ideas about how you plan to use the behaviors. Refer to the sentence starters in Appendix D of the book for suggestions. Consider whether and how to use electronic media (e-mail, teleconferences, web meetings, and so forth).

- Plan a sequence. (Be aware that the other person will be actively influencing you as well, so you may have to change your plan "on the fly.") Which of the tactics and specific behaviors will you begin with? Which ones will be most useful to you toward the conclusion?

- Troubleshoot. Think about how the conversation could go wrong and what you will do about it if that should happen, for example, "If the other person becomes angry or upset, then I will switch to Listening behaviors."

  If . . .

  If . . .

  If . . .

(Continued)

Planning Guide: Part 2 (continued)

- Focus on your next steps. What will you do if you achieve your goal? What will you do if you don't?

Set yourself up for success. For ideas, refer to page 100 in the book.

- What actions might you want to take before you meet with the other in order to create the conditions for success?

- What actions will you take at the end of the meeting to make sure that you and the other person are "on the same page" about the results and that any agreements between you will be implemented?

Planning Guide: Part 3

After the influence situation you planned for has taken place, ask yourself the following questions:

1. What worked well in the way I approached and handled the situation? What helped move us toward achieving my influence goal or acceptable alternative?

2. What was not effective in the way I approached and handled the situation? What made it difficult for us to achieve my goal or an acceptable alternative?

3. What was surprising to me during the actual situation? To what degree might I have anticipated that? How well did I handle it and how could I have handled it even better?

4. To what degree do I believe that the other person is satisfied with the outcome? How do I know this? What implementation issues may arise?

5. How might I have planned better for this situation?

6. What have I learned from this situation that I can apply to future influence opportunities?

7. What are some next steps to take with this person or around this issue with others?

Resources

Workshops and Seminars

Exercising Influence: Building Relationships and Getting Results. Barnes & Conti Associates, Inc., 800.835.0911, www.barnesconti.com.

Constructive Debate: Building Better Ideas. Barnes & Conti Associates, Inc., 800.835.0911, www.barnesconti.com.

Constructive Negotiation: Building Agreements That Work. Barnes & Conti Associates, Inc., 800.835.0911, www.barnesconti.com.

Inspirational Leadership: Encouraging Others to Do Great Things. Barnes & Conti Associates, Inc., 800.835.0911, www.barnesconti.com.

Facilitating Forward: Guiding Others Toward Results. Barnes & Conti Associates, Inc., 800.835.0911, www.barnesconti.com.

Graphic Facilitation (for meetings). The Grove Consultants, Inc., 800.494.7683, www.grove.com.

Facilitative Leadership (for meetings). Interaction Associates, Inc., 415.241.8000, www.interactionassociates.com.

Instrument

Myers-Briggs Type Indicator. Consulting Psychologists Press, Inc., 415.326.0255, www.mbti.com.

Additional Reading

Cialdini, Robert B. (1993). *Influence: The psychology of persuasion.* New York: William Morrow.

Emerson, Ralph Waldo. (1991). *Self-reliance.* New York: Bell Tower.

Fisher, Roger, & Sharp, Alan. (1998). *Getting it done: How to lead when you are not in charge.* New York: HarperCollins.

Gladwell, Malcolm. (2000). *The tipping point: How little things can make a big difference.* Boston: Little Brown.

Goleman, Daniel. (1998). *Working with emotional intelligence.* New York: Bantam Books.

Hogan, Kevin. (2004). *The psychology of persuasion: How to persuade others to your way of thinking.* Gretna, LA: Pelican Publishing.

Kouzes, James M., & Posner, Barry Z. (2005). *The leadership challenge* (3rd ed.). San Francisco: Jossey-Bass.

Maurer, Rick. (2002). *Why don't you want what I want? How to win support for your ideas without hard sell, manipulation, or power plays.* Houston, TX: Bard Press.

Tannen, Deborah. (1998). *The argument culture: Stopping America's war of words.* New York: Ballantine.